The World Is
Still Beautiful

STILL BEAUTIFUL

David Grandorge

Canalside Press

PLATES

Indiana Avenue III 1995

Melrose Avenue I 1999

Bermondsey I 2000

Kalmar I 2002

Paris I 2001

Paris II 2001

Hunstanton I 2002

Sugden House IV 2003

Lagos IV 2005

Lagos (Peak) 2005

Lagos (Lahda) 2005

Lagos I (Oshodi Market) 2005

Lagos II (Ebute Metta) 2005

Freetown III (Kroo Bay) 2005

Freetown I (David's Family) 2005

Alexandria I 2005

Coniston I 2006

Svalbard (Oxide River) 2007

Svalbard (Mine I) 2007

Svalbard (Coal Mountain) 2007

Svalbard (Cabin I) 2007

Svalbard (Blankets) 2007

Svalbard (EISCAT) 2007

Svalbard (Atlas) 2007

Svalbard (SvalSat II) 2007

Svalbard (SvalSat I) 2007

Svalbard (NASA) 2007

Kielder Forest 2008

Éveux I 2008

Orford Ness I 2010

Orford Ness V 2010

V&A I 2011

V&A II 2011

San Salvatore I 2014

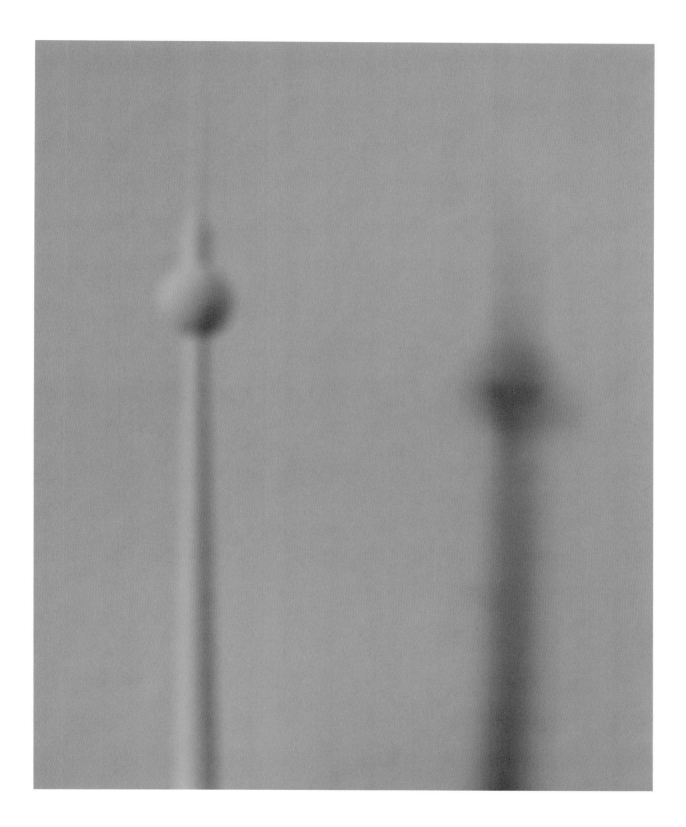

Fernsehturm I 2012

Oslo I 2013

Grand Union I 2013

Berlin (Rotaprint) I 2015

Vilnius I 2015

Ponary I 2015

Kaunus I 2015

Kedainiai I 2015

Zokniai I 2015

Zokniai VIII 2015

Zokniai XI 2015

Zokniai VI 2015

Zokniai X 2015

Riga II 2015

Vilnius IV 2015

Ignalina I 2015

Ignalina II 2015

Maardu IV 2016

Narva XIV 2016

Narva XVI 2016

Narva XVII 2016

Narva X 2016

Andja I 2016

Kurtna III 2016

Kohtle-Järve II 2016

Kohtle-Järve V 2016

Auvere I 2016

Tallinn II 2016

Luubnitsa I 2017

Mehikoorma I 2017

Lake Peipus I 2017

Jägala Waterfall II 2017

Gorsuch Place I 2016

Long Street I 2016

Zingaro I 2017

Dead Sea (near Wadi Mujib) I 2017

Siq al-Barid II 2017

Siq al-Barid I 2017

Siq Um Al Hiran to Wadi Araba I 2017

Siq Um Al Hiran to Wadi Araba II 2017

Siq Um Al Hiran to Wadi Araba III 2017

Tafileh Highway I 2017

Wadi Rum I 2017

Hejaz Railway I 2017

Desert Highway (Al Quweira) I 2017

Al Hasa Quarry I 2017

Quweira to Ma'an I 2017

Wadi Rum Village I 2017

Near Abu Al Luson I 2017

TEXTS

STILL BEAUTIFUL

Paul Shepheard

Millions of photographs swarm round the world every day. The cameras fit in your back pocket, and are called smart because they do everything for you. Their mode is AUTO, so you don't need a meter, they have anti-shake built in so you don't need a tripod. They store and edit their own product, so you don't need a darkroom. Their gift is stochastic: you point and shoot at what you see and they suck in images like a ramjet sucks in air and spew them out behind into the maw of the internet. Here are several thousand of the Trevi fountain in Rome; here, a truck load of the Catholic Church seen from the bridge in the middle of the red-light district in Amsterdam; and over here yet another pile, this time of Paris' great iron tower. Every minute, this representation of the world is further compounded, and stamped into the emerging mass. The result is that the world seems to have very few kinds of thing in it. It seems simple. It seems homogenous. Is that beautiful?

The world is an immensely complicated place. How did it become possible to interpret it so simply? There is a story that the crusades started with gangs setting off for the Levant on foot, and as they passed through towns and villages on the way they would be asked where they were going and they replied "to save Jerusalem! Join us!" And people would drop what they were doing, whatever it was, carving stones, tilling fields, cooking food, and fall into step. Eventually the gangs grew into crowds, all motivated by this simplest of pictures. It was as if the crusaders had carried smart phones with images of the cross. In the end it turned out that the warring armies were equally strong and that Jerusalem could not be held by expeditionary force and the simple picture faded away, but the story does not end there. The keepers of the Catholic faith in Portugal decided on an alternative strategy. This time they sent out ships around the African coast to try and discover a back way in to the holy land, hoping to find the site of the Garden of Eden. What they found instead was a whole new world, which needed a whole new map. And when the outlines of all the continents had been mapped, the next thing was to explore their interiors, and by so doing determine what the total contents of the world were. Put simply, that's what today's simple pictures are: images of the contents of the field of the New World.

The title of this collection, *Still Beautiful*, is enigmatic—it draws impetus from a renowned collection published in 1928 by Albert Renger-Patzsch called *The World Is Beautiful*—but which world is that? The pictures in here are so unfamiliar they could be of an alien planet. It is a place not even glimpsed in the blizzard of images coming from that smart-phone in your back pocket. The contents of the world are always in motion, always changing and evolving. This is partly because the desire of every species is to make it a better place for its own kind but also because it is in the nature of the material world to change. Gravity forged the elements and shaped the planets, and is still doing so. The keepers of the New World use the tools of reason, judgement and the law to try and hold the boundaries of the field in place but the contents keep escaping through holes in the fence. It's as though we, by which I mean the contents of the world both living and inert, are continuously straining to go feral. So what is beautiful?

There is a difference between an object and a thing. There are many ways of putting that notion but my way here is to say it is a distinction that resides in whether the object or thing in question is part of actuality itself, or part of our knowledge of it. After perusing this collection of images I'm now wondering whether there is a simple answer after all: the world could be an object and the New World could be a thing, but these pictures straddle the boundary. The boundary is the edge of the field. I have a vision of the photographer carrying heavy equipment right out to the edge of that boundary, setting up the image of the far side with detailed care and waiting for the right moment to fire the split second of exposure. But because these are pictures of change as much as they are pictures of places, I am tempted to say the boundary is also the one implicit in the double idea of space-time, and that these are also pictures of that. Amongst the stone and weather coloured actualities of the indescribable places—the raw beautiful—is the occasional lush image of a forest, of statuary, of a gilded interior, which comes as a shock of comfort to the living being; and there's the refined beautiful.

And also in there, as it always has been, is Africa. The incontrovertible veracity of these images of Lagos and Freetown, in which humanity is not just living alongside nature but is nature itself, remind me of the pictures bought back from the new world of the Americas in the seventeenth century. Far from smart, they are painstaking watercolours of the jolting difference of the ways life can be lived. They are not pictures of the noble savage, they are pictures of nature. They are about our occupations of the world, and how we do them and have done them. You can only see it if your thoughts are free because you have to ditch every vestige of simplicity to embrace complexity. The fields and boundaries in my extended metaphor are not a question of us and the 'other', they are about all of us: that is, the entire biomass, as well as the rocks and as well as the atmosphere. In other words, the total contents of the world.

WORLDLY AND PHOTOGRAPHIC BEAUTY

David Campany in conversation with David Grandorge

DC: *The World is Still Beautiful.* Your title is not as restrained as your photographs. And having not been to most of the places you have visited here, I can't tell if the beauty was observed in the world or produced in the act of describing it photographically, or if it's something in between. What's your feeling about this relation between worldly beauty and photographic beauty?

DG: Firstly, I should explain its origin. This working title originated in 2007. It was a phrase I commonly used to counter the melancholy I encountered in myself, and others, on realizing the possible consequences of climate change, resource depletion, loss of diversity, accumulation of wastes and so on. There was also a realization that our optimism about global co-operation was probably misplaced. This was exacerbated by my visit to Svalbard that year and also things I witnessed in West Africa in 2005.

The title was intended first as solace, then a rallying cry—an assertion that we can and should *still* recognize beauty in the world *despite* the fragility of our relationship to it.

It was also a reminder to myself to look more closely, to spend more time observing things that were neglected. Neglect is generally used in a pejorative sense, but it can be observed, in many cityscapes and landscapes, that neglect is the reason for a place's resilience to external economic and geo-political forces. I continue to be intrigued by this—what survives and what doesn't, in culture and nature.

The title is rather ebullient and long-winded in regard to the rather taut and laconic nature of my work. The book has been given, finally, the more compact title of *Still Beautiful*. It has a useful symmetry with my name and *Still* becomes a simple but ambiguous qualifier to our idea of beauty, its resilience as an idea, that it is still possible for us to recognize it.

With regard to the major thrust of your question, is the beauty observed in the world or is it produced in the act of describing the world photographically? It is primarily the former, but I hope, to a degree, that it exists in the latter. There are formal, structural, compositional, as well as political concerns evident in the pictures. I hope that the clarity in the description is able to provoke intellectual and emotional responses to what is, in essence, a painstakingly careful visual survey. The recognition of beauty in the photograph depends on the context in which it is seen and the scale at which it is shown. The relationship between world beauty and photographic beauty can be remote or closely coupled. It shifts from picture to picture.

DC: I guess this lands us already in the heart of the complicated overlay of beauty, melancholy, solace and the political. Photography—as record, as interpretation, as mute substitute—has particular ways of handling this overlay. Your images are 'taut and laconic', as you put it. Formal and reserved, and yet clearly open and generous too. Not always in the same way, or to the same degree, but there is a consistency to your approach, wherever you are in the world. Can you say a little about this?

DG: Consistency is important in any discipline to achieve a certain depth in the analysis of a subject or situation, but can become mundane if not challenged at intervals—intervals that, for me, are never self-determined but emerge at often difficult but rewarding moments when new pictorial or narrative problems present themselves. But an overall consistency was intended from the beginning. I had little interest in seriality but I was interested in how you could achieve the same type of picture qualities and picture facts when working in different contexts.

In my photographs there are varying degrees of consistency in my choice of subject matter, the type of pictorial space constructed, the composition of colour, the light in which a scene or object is shot and the resulting emotional temperature of the picture. To address them one by one:

- The choice of subject in my photographs is variable, but always very precise.
- The construction of the pictorial space is mostly consistent in that a 150mm lens is nearly always employed and in that I often use centred or frontal compositions, even in landscape situations. Oblique views are used when a situation absolutely dictates it.
- There is generally a precision in how objects are aligned within the frame. I am consistently interested in a quite narrow range of hues and try to arrange them in such a way that they are reconciled with each other.
- Light is determined by place, season, time of day and weather. I mostly shoot in diffuse light and in colder months. The colour and intensity of light is the most critical factor in achieving the simultaneous detachment from and engagement with the subject of the picture that I strive for.

DC: It's the balance of detachment and engagement that strikes me most here. Does photographic description demand restraint from the artist?

DG: For me, it does. Restraint, I think, is shown most clearly in my photographs of technical objects and landscapes. I try to temper their evident epic and exotic qualities, to render them in a more latent manner. This is dependent on the simplicity of framing and the tempered light in which the object or landscape is shot.

The balance of detachment and engagement is determined by one's knowledge of and empathy for a subject. It's important for me to be both generously intentioned and, if necessary, gently critical when making photographs, whatever the subject.

DC: May I return to your title, and in relation to your notion of generous intention? I'm reminded of the work of the German photographer Albert Renger Patzsch. His most famous book, an encyclopaedic collection of one hundred photographs of various things from various places, was given the emphatic and leading title *Die Welt ist Schön (The World is Beautiful)* by the publisher. Renger-Patzsch wanted the far more laconic and circumspect title *Die Dinge. Things*. Is your restraint an acceptance that while photographs show, they struggle to explain what they show or why they're showing it?

DG: Photographs have meaning by showing things, by making things visible in other contexts.

The ability of a photograph to show things depends on the context in which it is seen and the knowledge and insight of the person (or algorithm?) that is seeing it.

The restraint that characterises the pictures that I make is in part, as you posit, an acceptance of the struggle of the image to explain what is shown. In light of this predicament, I try to give an image as much authority as possible, to give it what we might call a strong constitution. I try to emphasize the stillness of both the camera and the thing or space photographed. As with images used for reconnaissance purposes or evidence in court, the photographs require additional information in order to be explained.

Restraint is also a reaction to the very special feeling one has on arriving in a new place, a zone. There is a desire to remain grounded, whilst still communicating one's affection, empathy or fascination for the subject.

The tension between the title "Still Beautiful" and the content is intended. A title creates an expectation about the content. It is enjoyable and useful to play with this expectation. The title is more postscript than intention.

RECONNAISSANCE

David Grandorge

When J.G. Ballard was asked, "Do you think that there is a moral purpose to your fiction?" he replied,

> "I am not sure about that. I see myself more as a kind of investigator, a scout who is sent on ahead to see if the water is drinkable or not."[1]

I most often inhabit a very small part of the world. Its most private boundary is the room in which I am now writing. The room has a north-facing window, always open to allow for the circulation of air, warm or cool. The space is unheated. On the desk, there are two ageing computers tethered to a tower of hard drives, usually lying dormant, but sometimes fired up to retrieve important visual or other information. A coffee cup, cigarettes, lighter and ashtray also rest on this surface, with books crammed together on shelves above and the floor below.

The room is in a house alive with the sound of teenage children, my own and others. Outside, a street lined with garages, a hinterland of a park in East London. Beyond that, an old and mercantile city through which I travel on foot or bicycle to places of work, consumption and recreation. I have never driven a car. This has helped keep my world relatively small.

Occasionally, I have been privileged to travel to and document, through photography, a larger world—physically remote and culturally distinct from the city where my beliefs, attitudes and behavior have been formed. This has been enabled by the rapid expansion and reduced cost of travel by air and the passport I travel with, (allotted to me through an accident of birth), that allows me to pass through borders with comparative ease. Beyond that, I rely on others, strangers and friends, to transport me by road or track.

The photographs that accompany these words were made during short yet immersive trips to West Africa, the Arctic, the Baltic states and Jordan. They are concerned, in the first instance, with how pictorial problems related to the representation of landscape can be solved. They are portraits of landscapes subjected to significant geopolitical pressures. I try to stay clear of political topicality, as these pressures ebb and flow over a protracted timescale. Nevertheless, a consideration of the forces acting upon these situations, and the effect these have on those living there, exposes one, in a very direct way, to the pain of others.

The photographs were made by exposing light on to film. The expense of using sheet film and the weight of the view camera leads one to be more particular in choosing subjects to document and addressing how they might be composed within a frame. It affords a greater clarity in the depiction of an object or scene. Some of the subjects of the pictures were chanced upon, some the result of pilgrimages taken. Together, they can be understood, like Ballard's assertion, as a form of *reconnaissance*.

My trip to West Africa in July 2005 was the first time I had travelled outside of Europe or America. On arriving at the airport in Lagos, I was taken in a diplomatic people carrier with three armed guards to the British Council compound situated on Lagos Island in the south of the city. The level of protection afforded me seemed unnecessary, but at this moment in time, the Foreign Office deemed Lagos to be the second most dangerous city for a British citizen to visit after Baghdad in Iraq. On this first rather hectic and stressful journey through the city, weaving through dense traffic on an elevated highway, I noticed two urban-scaled settlements below, a busy open-air market and a grouping of huts on stilts sitting in the lagoon. I would return to these sites three days later to document them, again accompanied by three armed guards.

Lagos I (Oshodi Market) 2005

Oshodi Market was established in 1860 whilst Nigeria was under British colonial rule. Slave trading took place there in its early years, mainly for the sale of slaves to America, even though the British Parliament had abolished the practice in 1807. I was unaware of its history or its contemporary relevance as I set up my tripod on the highway overlooking this scene. My intention was to make an image of an urban space that was typical to cities around the world, to show something equivalent. Seen from above, markets have the quality of a mat or a tapestry. It was this universal quality that attracted me. Hustle and bustle is evident in the foreground of the picture, yet activity within the market is concealed as the stalls are densely configured in order to protect traders and shoppers from the searing equatorial sun. Breaking up the frame is a long stair that connects to a pedestrian bridge spanning a wide road at the edge of the market, along which yellow buses jostle for space. An advert for Paracetamol, 'Dr Meyer's PAINKIL', is conspicuous on the horizon.

The market no longer exists. It was demolished (nearly ten years after this photograph was taken) in January 2015 as a result of a Lagos State Government directive.

Lagos II (Ebute Metta) 2005

The second photograph taken was an overview of the Makoko settlement on Ebute Metta Water that, like Oshodi Market, was established in the nineteenth century. The settlement has grown over time, more rapidly in recent years to a population of approximately 85,000 and is viewed by the Lagos authorities as a slum. It looked to me (naively?) to possess the qualities of a well-designed and self-regulating entity. I was attracted to its village-like quality and the elegant fact of the simple huts raised just above the water on timber poles. The resulting picture has a surprising stillness. Electricity infrastructure is just visible on the horizon. There is intermittent evidence of occupancy, latent and apparent.

The settlement has not fared well since this photograph was taken. A great amount of waste (human, plastic and oil) has accumulated in the lagoon and there have been damaging outbreaks of fire of unknown origin in the settlement itself and in timber mills at the lagoon's edge. Despite many threats to its existence, it remains resilient.

Svalbard (Coal Mountain) 2007

I would next travel to a remote landscape in September 2007 (just after the EU wide ban on smoking in public buildings and just before the launch of Apple's first 'smart' phone), to Svalbard in the Arctic Circle. I was there at the invitation of the Norwegian architects Brendeland & Kristoffersen. They had asked me to document three carefully designed terraced houses of varying girth that had been built for the Store Norske mining company in the settlement of Longyearbyen. The mountain ranges that surround the settlement have deep seams of coal that have been exploited since the beginning of the twentieth century. Small mountains of extracted coal sit in a field of black that stretches to the harbour where a gantry crane loads it on to ships that will finally transfer it to the Norwegian mainland. It was satisfying to make a picture in a place usually defined by snow and ice that was almost all black.

Svalbard (Oxide River) 2007

Svalbard was of strategic importance during the Second World War. German forces occupied the archipelago from 1943 so that they could establish meteorological stations there. Previously, in 1941, the Allied forces had evacuated its inhabitants and destroyed existing settlements and installations. The bombing left still visible red scars (like stigmata) on the shale-covered faces of the mountainside, a result of fires fuelled by the coal seams below. Iron oxide continues to leak from these scars. When the snow melts, iron oxide residues form trails that describe the path of water during the melt.

Svalbard (Nasa) 2007

Svalbard hosts a range of important scientific installations including the EISCAT radar, the Max Planck antenna field and the Global Seed Vault. Upon a plateau above the airport, sits the Svalsat satellite ground station. The site is difficult to get to as no vehicular access is allowed from a point three miles downslope. Arriving on the plateau, I was reminded of the following words by Hilla Becher:

"We do not travel to these places for pleasure. As they are not meant for strangers, they have a very intensive effect, which in my case imparts a very positive and adventurous atmosphere. They possess neither flower borders, nor attractions. It is indeed rather special to arrive in an area that is real, because it is what it is. It neither exhibits itself nor does it make itself artificially popular. It is neither attractive nor inviting for strangers, conforms to no notions."[2]

I photographed a number of the radomes on the site, the most significant of which is owned and operated by NASA to support its Earth Observing System. The photographic intention here, common to much of my work, was to render this extraordinary object in the most ordinary way. The space between the object and edge of frame was carefully chosen. The mundane quality of the skip on the left-hand side of the frame serves as a matter-of-fact counterpoint to the monumentality of the complex technological object and the epic landscape in which it is placed. The object is what it is.

The SvalSat site seemed orderly, well managed and a project characterized by non-partisan global co-operation. In the age of information, cracks have appeared in this order. There have been at least two breaches of the site's cyber security, where hackers have sought to take control of satellites, though this was not achieved. Furthermore, the Norwegian journalist Bard Wormdal has alleged that SvalSat has been used for military intelligence, thereby breaching the Svalbard Treaty. He alleges that this has included the illegal use of satellite imagery of Libya by Italian military intelligence and of Afghanistan and North Korea by American military intelligence.

Svalbard is also widely known as a frontier of research into the effects of climate change. While I was there, scientists were measuring extents of a number of glacier retreats in the region. This phenomenon is most extensively measured by sensing equipment orbiting the earth, but it is still deemed important to make observations on the ground. I met one of the scientists in the only bar in town at the end of her research period. After I had ascertained from her the subject and scope of her work, I asked, "How did the measurements go?" "I think I need a drink before I can tell you about them" she replied. She and her colleagues had just measured the greatest summer retreat of ice ever recorded and had already reported their findings to a number of organisations, including the UN. This and other measured records of the decrease in the volume of ice in the Arctic have been broken a number of times since. How does one react to such knowledge?

In "Facing Gaia" (2017), the French anthropologist Bruno Latour discusses several typical human reactions to climate change, from those who live in a parallel world of denial (Trump, et al), to those who acknowledge it and think that we should solve the problem by exerting greater control over the Earth system (geo-engineering), to those who don't think the problem can be solved and sink into melancholia, then depression, and to those who think that collective action is still possible and could find us a way out of our predicament. Latour tells us that, "What could have been just a passing crisis has turned into a profound alteration of our relation to the world."[3] He further points out that "an alteration of the relation to the world" is the scholarly term for madness.[4]

Gerhard Richter addressed climate change without equivocation in his notes of 1st June, 1992. He wrote:

".... the realization of climatic damage and the prospect of a climatic catastrophe creates fear, but no effective action towards changing it. On the contrary, fear is only a sign of our certainty that we can change nothing, and to palliate our fear we go in for displacement activities that make not the slightest possible difference; just like our ancestors, who faced up to Nature, armed with nothing but prayers and sacrificial offerings."[5]

Richter words were very much in my thoughts when, in 2013, I exhibited fifteen works from the Svalbard series in an exhibition entitled "Without Sun" at Peter Von Kant in Deptford. The opening was attended by the Lithuanian curators Jonas Zukauskas and Jurga Daubaraite. Later, in 2015, they would invite me to document a number of sites in the Baltic States as part of the Baltic Pavilion project for the 2016 Venice Biennale.

I asked a fellow photographer and friend, Jonathan Lovekin to join me in undertaking this endeavour. There were three reasons for this. Firstly, he had made work in Estonia before and he understood some of the ground over which we would travel. We would be working in difficult, sometimes perilous weather conditions and, as we would sometimes be documenting energy & military infrastructure without permission, there could be threats to personal health, security and liberty. Secondly, the scope of the project required more than one set of eyes. Thirdly, we have always talked to each other about our work. This would be a chance to have this dialogue whilst making it.

Zokniai XI 2015

We visited the Baltic States on four occasions between March 2015 and March 2017. The third stop on our first trip was a former Soviet airfield at Zokniai in Lithuania. The Russian military abandoned the airfield in 1993 on the condition that it would not be used for military purposes again. Subsequently, the former hangars for Soviet jet fighters were used (as they were the cheapest option) to store biomass, a useful, but low value by-product of the harvesting of birch trees. Birch trees have self-seeded on the grass that grows over the hangars, originally intended to hide the facility from western military reconnaissance planes.

Putin's continued and continuing attempts do destabilize the Western democratic model have included incursions into Baltic air space and the deployment of troops along the Russian border with the Baltic States. Since 2004, NATO has used the Zokniai airfield and other sites in Latvia and Estonia on a provisional basis. A number of NATO members are involved in the task of policing the air space of the Baltic states with different members taking responsibility every three or four months. This task is ongoing, expensive and probably necessary.

After coming online in 1983, the formerly Soviet owned nuclear power plant at Ignalina in Lithuania produced abundant low-carbon electrical power for the whole Baltic region for over twenty years. Significantly, it employed the same Soviet designed RMBK 1500 reactor that failed with catastrophic consequences at Chernobyl in 1986. It was this fact and the fragility of the reactor hall's containment building that prompted the European Union to make its closure a condition of Lithuania's accession agreement. When reactor two was finally put to rest on December 31st 2009, the long and arduous process of decommissioning began.

It was during this phase that the Baltic Pavilion curators were able to negotiate access for us to its interior (the bureaucratic task was of Soviet proportions). After passing through security checks with military and administrative staff, shedding our clothes and dressing in white suits that were intended to protect us from any residual radiation in the facility, we were able to enter the depths of the plant. We made photographs of the reactor hall and floor, the turbine hall and condensers and were finally taken to the control room. It had echoes, as all control rooms do, of "Dr. Strangelove".

This picture of the de-commissioned and electrically isolated control desk has a claustrophobic feel. The crop is deliberately tight. The gauges at the top of the frame now tell us nothing of the immense heat that was once created. The buttons on the desk, that once controlled the depth of the fuel rod in the reactor, now had the quality of something found in a bingo hall. It must be noted that the colours of the control desk and panel are not dissimilar to those used by IBM in the 1970s and 80s. Our guide told us that when operational, the control room was full of operators chain-smoking cigarettes, due to their having to make critical decisions at least every two minutes. In contemporary power and industrial plants, this part of the operation is run by algorithms, as are the planes we fly in. Information and analogue technologies have merged.

Auvere I 2016

With nuclear power sidelined, the Baltic countries have had to adopt higher carbon technologies. Oil shale has a long history in Estonia. It is extracted from surface or underground mines. This picture was taken on our third trip to the Baltics in March 2016 at the edge of an oil shale-fired power plant in northeast Estonia near the Russian border. My passport was in the hands of an Estonian Border guard at the moment I released and closed the lens shutter.

What is shown is a partial view of a mountain of ash, the residue left over after shale oil is burnt. It is part of the 4,500,000 tons of waste material that is deposited every year, after washing, in ash storage lagoons. The ash mountain, dusted with snow, has separating layers within it that allow water to drain into the surrounding moat. Even though the temperature was about minus 10°C when the photograph was taken, the toxic water in the moat did not freeze due to the heat it had absorbed from the pile of ash. The portrait format was employed to emphasize the different states of water and exploit their reflective qualities. These qualities, combined with a long exposure time, take part of the image near to abstraction.

Dead Sea (Near Wadi Mujib) I 2017

The final photograph of landscape presented is a horizontally emphatic view of the Dead Sea taken from Jordan looking to Israel in January 2017. Through this body of water pass two significant demarcations, the 1949 Armistice agreement line that runs west to east, and the 1994 Treaty Line that runs north to south. Its shores are situated at the lowest point on Earth, more than 400m below sea level. This point is becoming lower with each passing year due to increased demand for fresh water in Jordan (and elsewhere upstream in Israel and Syria) and the damming of the three tributaries that run into it. It has resulted in dangerous sinkholes that are visible on the newly exposed shoreline. It is a barometer for the region in many ways.

So, is this reconnaissance? It feels like it.

Landscapes, if documented with precision and intentionality, can reveal something of both their history and their physical attributes at the time that the document was made. These attributes will always be in flux. Reconnaissance helps us to become more aware of our dependence on resources and infrastructure, even if it cannot help us to break this dependence. It can also help us to embrace material culture and to understand and feel the ground beneath our feet. Reconnaissance reconnects us with many actualities, but most importantly, reminds us that the world is *still* beautiful.

1   "An Investigative Spirit", an interview between Travis Elborough and
    J.G. Ballard conducted in 2006, published as an end piece to Ballard's
    novel High-Rise, Fourth Estate, 2014 edition.

2   Hilla Becher in conversation with Heinz-Norbert Jocks, featured in,
    Susanne Lange, "Bernd and Hilla Becher, Life and Work", MIT Press,
    2007, p.211

3   Bruno Latour, "Facing Gaia, Eight Lectures on the New Climatic
    Regime", Polity Press, 2017, p.9

4   Bruno Latour, ibid, p.10

5   Gerhard Richter, "The Daily Practice of Painting", MIT Press, 1998,
    p.242

The World is Still Beautiful
Rake Visningsrom, Trondheim, Norway
23 March - 21 April 2013

Without Sun
Peter Von Kant Deptford, London
25 October - 7 December 2013

Ground *with Jonathan Lovekin*
Baltic Pavilion Beta Version, 12 Vilnius Art Biennale
2015

Ground *with Jonathan Lovekin*
Baltic Pavilion, 15th Venice Architecture Biennale
2016

Ground *with Jonathan Lovekin*
AA Gallery & RIBA Future Practice Gallery, London
1 - 25 March 2018

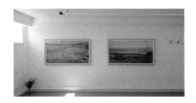

Landscapes of Variable Temperature
Six Second Gallery, Dalston, London
20 - 29 April 2018